It's Okay Not to Be Okay

Addressing the Concept of Toxic Positivity

By Katie Musleh

Illustrated By Prexie Beland

Published by The Elite Lizzard Publishing Company
Written by Katie Musleh and Illustrated by Prexie Beland.
2022

Everyone feels different kinds of emotions from time to time.

Sometimes we feel happy or sad, angry or mad.

Scared or excited, disappointed or delighted.

Relieved or embarrassed, silly or even nervous.

What's important to know is that these feelings are OKAY.

Happy or sad, angry or mad, scared or excited, disappointed or delighted, relieved or embarrassed, silly or even nervous!

Feelings, good or bad, tell us what we need everyday.

If you are feeling sad, maybe you need a hug.

If you are feeling lonely, a friend to play with.

If you are angry, maybe you need to count to ten and take deep breaths until you calm down again.

Bored? Try playing a game! Draw what's outside your window...

...or go biking down the lane.

Now, there's one important rule that YOU NEED TO KNOW.

It's never, ever OKAY to pretend to feel happy when you are feeling low.

To feeling better again, our emotions need to be EXPRESSED.

Not bottled up in a glass or buried deep in our chest.

Everyone feels down sometimes and feeling down is OKAY. There is a time and place for everything and feeling down is the same.

So, whenever you feel sad, remember this saying...

"IT'S OKAY TO NOT BE OKAY" There's no need for play pretending!

The End

NOTE TO PARENTS

This book is meant address the concept of toxic positivity in a child friendly manner.

Toxic positivity can be defined as the overgeneralization of happiness and a state of optimism that causes an individual's authentic emotional experience to become denied, minimized and ultimately, invalidated.[1]

It is crucially important to teach your kid that feeling negative emotions is okay and should not be suppressed. A child should not feel like they have to pretend to be happy when they are not. Furthermore, popularized phrases such as "just be positive" are not healthy ways to address negative emotions.

---

[1] *SOURCE: TANGLAW MENTAL HEALTH*

NOTE TO PARENTS

In fact, they can often result in the child feeling like their emotions or experiences are invalid and even lead them to believe that that they should always be happy.

Instead, it is important to reassure your child that it's okay to experience negative emotions. A good example of a phrase you could use is the very title of this book.

It is highly suggested that parents educate themselves about toxic positivity and how it can negatively impact kids so they can avoid unintentionally teaching it to their child.

HOW TO AVOID TOXIC POSITIVITY

To help you address your child's emotions in a healthier way, here are some examples of phrases you can use instead of more invalidating ones.

Instead of saying...	Say...
"You"ll get over it."	"It's hard but I believe in you."
"Don't be so negative!"	"It's okay to feel bad sometimes"
"Failure is not an option..."	"Failure is part of growth."

SOURCE: TANGLAW MENTAL HEALTH

HOW TO AVOID TOXIC POSITIVITY

Instead of saying...

Say...

"Always look on the bright side!"

"It can be difficult to see the good in this situation, but we'll make sense of it when we can."

"Think happy thoughts!"

"Things can get really tough, I am here for you."

"It could be worse."

"Sometimes we experience bad things. How can I support you?"

SOURCE: TANGLAW MENTAL HEALTH

About the Author

Katie Musleh is a psychology undergraduate student at the University of Waterloo.

She is passionate about spreading awareness surrounding mental health and stigma, with plans to enter the mental health field.

She is the creator of Lit*tle Bit of Lemons* - a blog she started to spread mental health awareness and talk about the ways that she has healed from her own trauma.

In her spare time, she enjoys playing the piano, thrift shopping,

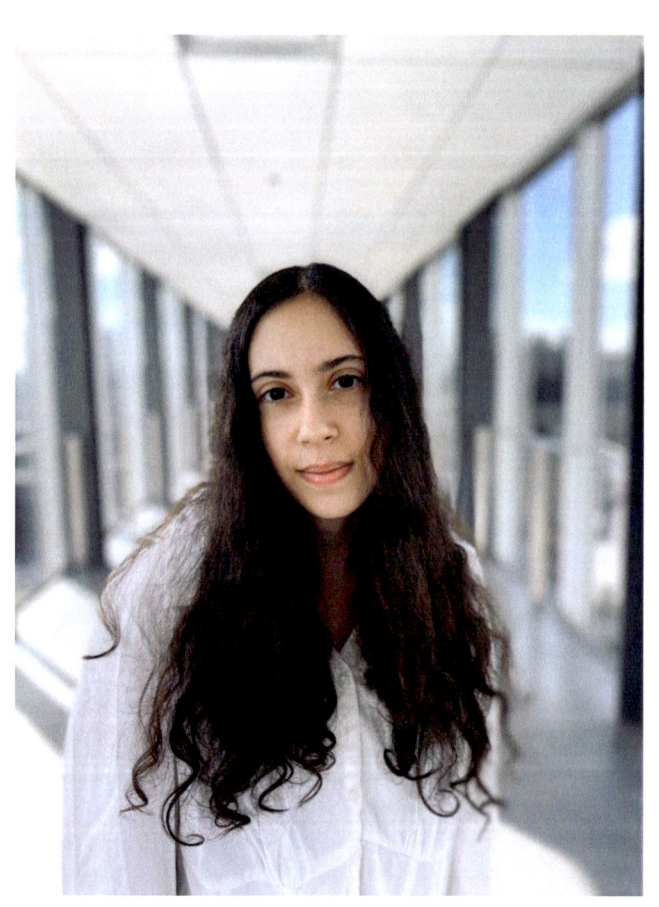

eating out with friends, and exploring the city of Waterloo.